Notes From Paradise

poems

Elaine Heveron

Plain View Press, LLC
1101 W 34th Street, STE 404

www.plainviewpress.c~
Austin, TX 7

ISBN: 978-1-63210-103-7
ebook ISBN: 978-1-63210-104-4
Library of Congress Control Number: 2023945144

Cover art *Girls Night Out* by Stuart Glazer
Cover design by Pam Knight

We Find Healing In Existing Reality
Plain View Press is a 47-year-old issue-based literary publishing house. Our books result from artistic collaboration between writers, artists, and editors. Over the years we have become a far-flung community of humane and highly creative activists whose energies bring humanitarian enlightenment and hope to individuals and communities grappling with the major issues of our time—peace, justice, the environment, education and gender.

Notes From Paradise

poems

elaine heveron
9/22/23

Elaine Heveron

Previous Collections of Poetry
by Elaine Heaveron

Email to Cleveland (Plain View Press, 2007)
Not Every Woman Swooned (Plain View Press, 2009)

*To my superb husband
and exquisite poet, Louis Faber,
(https://anoldwriter.com)
who whipped up delicious healthy meals and
provided technical and psychic support for all the
weeks it took me to choose,
revise and re-write the poems for this book.*

Thank you, love.

Contents

Jazz, Books, Jive

Jazz Festival Haiku—June 2010

At Home
Writing room finished:
two desks, two chairs, two journals.
Let's hope the words flow.

On The Way
In the car he fumes
lambasting other drivers.
(Only she can hear!!)

People Watching I
Every woman owns
a dress she saves to dazzle.
Then that night arrives.

In Line
Everyone asks us
where we found our folding chairs.
We unfold replies.

On Stage
Red conga drums stand
tall and skinny, double mics
An ti ci pa tion!

Somi at Max
We wait in the rain
for Somi to sing at Max.
She sings me to tears.

Live
Live music—so great!
Hard to capture on record
(They still say *record*.)

People Watching II
I saw it tonight;
I will never understand—
A brunette goes blonde!

Herbie at Eastman
E- lec- tron- ic- a!
Herbie, what happened to you?
Thank God for the drums.

Xerox VIP Tent
The champagne is free—
we both sip it way too fast.
Christ Church concert waits.

John Taylor at Christ Church
Musicians drift in
for John Taylor's piano.
One by one they stay.

Big Tent
Tea in the Big Tent
Scottish Reggae West Coast Jazz
Horn-guitar ballads!

Vending
Coca cola stand—
vitamin water costs more;
Diet Coke for her.

Very Late in the Big Tent
With one drunken foot,
woman kicks bar stool over—
trips Security.

Java's
Java's table free!
All sandwiches are gourmet.
Mmm mmm mmm mmm mmm.

Sixth Night
Wednesday fest day six:
we're all way tired tonight,
planning day seven.

Participation
Stage lights blink at me;
I take leave of audience.
Conga line forming!

Shawl
Bring a nice long shawl—
late night air might chill your soul.
Wrap 'round your shoulders.

Kilbourn Hall Alley Line I
Kilbourn folks cue up
eat standing there outside—
(next to port-a-johns!)

Kilbourn Hall Alley Line II
Brick walkway, brick wall.
We put our trust in mortar.
Echoes bounce across.

Joe Locke
Joe Locke rides the vibes.
We all return home again—
Ken-ny Wash-ing-ton!

Women's Shoes
Backless thin high heels—
they do not support her feet!
(Does my envy show?)

To Tote or Not to Tote
I should have brought that;
I should not have brought so much!
(Baggage is my name!)

Year Seven
John comes out on stage
Nuge holds up seven fingers.
The crowd goes wild.

Groupies
Beth/Michelle arrive
always the first two in line
How does that happen?

A Club
At last a waitress smiles,
asks what we would like to eat.
Now I can't decide.

Public Rest Rooms
I have had my fill
of waiting in rest room lines.
But the jazz, Jazz, JAZZ!

Max of Eastman Place
White haired man in hall
wears a bright colorful vest
We are all Jazz Age.

High School Bands/Free Stage
High school band plays on—
Jazz Street fills up end to end.
Where to go from here?

Sean Jones I
Keyboard, horns, bass, drums—
a hot quintet plays on stage.
Can't bear much more joy.

Sean Jones II
"Cloud Nine Obsession"
is about addictive love.
Shoot me some of that!

Sean Jones III
The band has amp problems
Piano, trumpet play on
Drummer checks his cell.

Sean Jones IV
Button trumpet slays
Sean Jones takes it to the MAX
Bedtime? When was that?

Second Last Night
Two evenings to go
Booker T and the MG's
I can barely wait!

Jazz and Blues

Alison Burns is singing
How Long Has This Been
   Going On?
in Montage and as I turn
my head away from watching
her sing, turning instead
toward the audience,
I see a glassiness
in the eyes of a stranger—
and it is *her* response
to this song I love
that tears at me.

A man, on the other side
of the room shakes his head,
ever so slightly, as if to rid
himself of a thought, or
a memory—which
comes out, nonetheless,
like a sigh—his lower lip
a trembling ledge—
and I wish I could put
these two people together.

Dress Nightgown

I buy this long
soft yellow dress—
what a great find!

It's mostly hemp,
but partly silk—
isn't that divine!

But, uh-oh,
it's see-through,
I now realize.

I demote it
from dress
to nightgown.

That evening,
I wear it to bed.
My husband—he
looks so surprised.

My Secret Afternoon Delight

Once a week I remove my wedding rings,
toss them in a tray on the vanity,
pin my hair up away from my face—
a younger look if I say so myself.
A friend of mine got me into this—
I never thought I would do it.
But a pandemic's uncertainty
brings things out in people—
　　both good and bad, I know.
It is not boredom; I'm never bored.
It is not the money either, truly it's not.
I just need to mix things up—
　　to keep it alive.
I rub a little oil on my hands,
press them into the flour and water,
add the sourdough I've been feeding
all week, now kneading like a pro.
My husband loves
my fresh baked loaves.

A Boy on a Beach

You're not exactly a boy,
a young man maybe fresh
from college—are you here
for the season? Is this
your summer show—you
dancing, twirling round in the
sand in your red shirt, baggy black
pants, your goateed chin in the air.
It's not as if we wouldn't have
noticed that pointed beard had
it not been jabbing the sky
as you leap in the air.
From whence does your joy
spring on this dark rainy day?
Did someone say yes to
the question you almost
dared not ask? Is that lone
swimmer now earnestly
high crawling to shore
headed for you?

A Song for You

I could've tossed that box of snapshots, still sealed since we moved
here, taking up prime real estate
in the front hall closet. But there's
something eerie about photos—
how they hold a moment up
to your face like evidence—
proving or challenging your
memory. You might see
an intimate glance between
two people you thought were
new to each other—or two people
laughing or frowning a bit too hard
at someone unseen, someone outside
of the photo. Wait—that would be me.

Leon Russell looked right in my eyes
one night at a concert. I had a second-
row seat, high-speed Black and White
film, a 400 mm Nikon lens. He let me
capture his eyes, usually shaded by
sunglasses or that wide-brimmed
white hat he wore. I kept shooting
and shooting and, well, he let me.
But you miss things while you're
focused on taking photos. Like,
what was he singing just then?
I don't know. I cannot recall.
But we were alone and he
was singing that song for me.

For Lou (Valentine's Day 2011)

Although I suspect (and have
often said that) you could have
loved anyone with your cheerful
optimism, fearlessness, and joy,
it does not diminish the
astonishing fact that
you allowed yourself
to choose to love me.
I was just a friend
of a friend, who agreed
to spend one dinner hour
with you. You were full of
gab for a guy unfamiliar with
the single life. You laid out your
long-winded jokes. Did I laugh
or groan as I shook my head? I
cannot recall. Your website photo
did you no favor. Your dark poems
there frightened me a bit, but that
heaviness was nowhere to be found
across the table at dinner, or later
at coffee, or at the next six hundred
and twenty-seven dinners we shared
before you married me for good.
You took my imaginary lover
and wrestled him down
to the ground.

Conversation

Hey, Hold on.
Please—can we talk?
Right here above the trees—
   just the two of us?

You've got some swagger
   over planet earth!
We need to have a
   real conversation—
not this mockingbird
ever changing tweet.

Look at us!
Look at you—
   always dancing through conflict,
   departing through courtship.
I thought you were fearless!

Look at me!
Can't you see you're
   my heart's desire.
There's nothing to fear
   but gravity!

Let's get to the Real Real.
Come on now—okay?
Okay.
You go first.

How Could This Be?

How could this be?
My expansive desolation
   ends with technology.
The miracle I waited for—
   when, where, how—
   what was the code?
How would I find my peace
   within the flock of the hearing?
My paradise of endless
   live music was lost
   to near deafness.
No more music, not even
   background on TV sitcoms.
I would mute the high-range noise.
It was frostbite to the slight
   remains of my hearing.
But now, this week—
   the thrill of birthing sonar
in the deep: one click; high tech
   I can hear you.
Cautiously I pop a CD in the player.
   Tears rise in my eyes.
Music is news to my kitten.
   Paradise returned to me.

Dream Journal III

April 12
I wake up from a dead-end dream—
trying to remember the last name
of someone I never knew,
trying to recall a recipe
for something I never baked.

April 15
Sweet Mistakes
Vance has an amazing relationship
with his voice, "Are we going to do this?"
he asks Ellis. Then out it comes, with
the force of all heaven and earth,
they sang our wedding song to us,
right there in the club at our table.

It's May.
It's mid-May
It's post Lilac Festival, May 20
And still I reach for my gloves
to go for a walk.
It's late May here in Rochester.

May 28
I'm gonna' love you 'til nobody else
loves you come feign or come sigh.
Happy together in indecent weather
Oh, won't you be mine?

Amber

Though she'll be on her feet all day,
Amber stands while we catch up.
Her eyes widen as she tells her stories,
as if her news is news to her as well,
as if she, with her teething-ring earrings,
rosy cheeks and new blue hair, is one of
her friends who are waiting for her here.

She shares some complex tribulations
with no indignation, but with humble
pride in her children's burgeoning lives—
the way one does with old friends.
In spite of many enigmatic woes—
she lets loose a deep soothing laugh—
as only the enlightened can do.

She knows our hippie home
as well as her own, and goes at
her work like a balloon twister. She
shuffles our stuff, washes, vacuums and
dusts. She brightens the air with essential
oils. In her hands, our laundered linen
napkins become a nest of exotic birds.
Later, we return to a freshened haven.
Gratefully, we grin, "We've been Ambered."

Don't Pay the Ferryman

If you're planning to ferry across the lake from
Toronto to Rochester, it might help to know:
The Baker Street Bakery is on Park Avenue.
The Park Avenue Bike Shop is on Monroe
Avenue. Lake Shore Record Exchange is
neither at the Lake or the Shore. The
Beale Street bar is on South Avenue.
Tony's Culver Atlantic Service Station
used to be at Culver and Atlantic but
now is at Winton Road and Empire.

Maria's Mexican Restaurant is in a Church
Corpus Christi Church is in a Music Hall,
and Pomodoro Italian Restaurant is in an
old blade factory next to the railroad, or
it once was. White hot dogs are made here
with pork, people grill them 'till they're black.

But "The White Hots" are a jazzy blues band—
they play at "The Little" and in Pultneyville.
"The Little" is a five-screen indie movie theater,
serving popcorn with real butter, and a café
serving espresso, light meals, dessert, and wine.
With frequently rotating art exhibits, and live
local music most evenings, it's the place to be.

Charlotte beach (pronounced "Char-LOT") is
this side of our shared Lake Ontario. On a clear
day, we can see you on the other side, Toronto.

Oh, and we sold the ferry. But come anyway!
Welcome to Rochester.

CD Release Party

I tried to tell the Sound Man that
the music was too loud. He shook
his head, pointing to his ears. I
said: "THE MUSIC IS TOO LOUD!"

I could not discern the lyrics
so I watched the players play,
figured I'd read them later
from the liner notes in the case.

I told the CD sales dude, as we left
before the end, the music was loud
and garbled. He blamed it on The
Mission. He said "It's the acoustics, you
know, in here!" I looked around the little
old church, which holds a hundred folks or so.
"Hey, man," I said, "it's not a stadium, you know."

"Hope you can hear when you get outside,"
he smiled, handing me my change. I thought,
"My hearing is already abysmal, my man.
But you might still have some time."

In the car, I slit open the shrink wrap,
pulled the leaflet out from the sleeve,
to read the lyrics that I could not hear—
but there was nothing inside to read.

Paintings of People

Our home is filled with
paintings of people—
an abstract blue-faced
man with spiked thick hair
sips coffee. I hang a shy blue
Joni Mitchell-like portrait
to his right for company.
A wind-blown child holds a
tattered scarf over his mouth,
as he stares at the viewer. Two
people, dancing a little too far
apart, consider becoming a couple.
A floating Chagall-like clown swims
high in the sky with star-filled eyes.
A wise old man, one palm inside
the other, holds his pain in his lap.
A public market boy, joyously seizes
each day. He has enough joy to share.
A relaxed but dressed up woman glances
off to the side, talking with jazz hands
in the air. Every time we walk in the
room, it feels like we just missed a
hilarious story or great bit of news.

They hail us like taxis
from gallery walls where
they hang. We are not young,
we tell them, we met so late in life—
too late to have our own children.
Then we agree, to buy one more,
and one more, nodding, writing
our checks, carrying them home.

Keyboard

The odd thing was that I'd just
arrived home from being at Sound
Source—playing with all the piano
keyboards, listening to John C,
the salesman my brother told me
to see—and my phone is ringing.
It's Carol. Hey, I just need to vent,
she says. Hey, I say—interrupting her—
Do you have a keyboard you want to sell?
She says: I have one I'll give to you.
I say, No, seriously; I'm looking for
a keyboard—you're out of a job—I'll
pay you! Do you know if it's a full
keyboard, or just 66 keys? She says,
I don't know—the whole thing, like
always. You plug it into the computer.
I say, Oh, I don't want to plug it into
a computer; I want one I can plug
right into the wall. She says, I thought
you said you needed a keyboard for
your computer! I say, No, I need a
keyboard so I can learn to play piano.
What did you want to vent about?
She says: jobs on Craigslist are a scam.
I say, yeah—the keyboards there
aren't any good either. Okay,
see you tomorrow, she says.

Blue Hand

for Brian Heveron-Smith

Slap this blue-gloved hand onto the rim
of your plastic-topped dumbek and know
that I'm there, laughing in your audience,
getting all your jokes. (Forget that I am
old and can't hear half the time. There's
a 23-year-old inside me, pleased to *not*
get carded at nightclubs, and say what
you will about high heels on women:
I never wore them. But some men
thought I was hot enough to call
the next day, and the day after
that, and to keep my phone
number long after his *little*
black book was tossed by
his late-in-life first wife.)
It only takes one person to
put his hands together first.
Applause sounds unanimous,
but there's one dude who gets it
going, a second or so before all the
rest. That man there doesn't care if
no one else ever claps, since he's having
a grand old time. Give that guy a big hand!
C'mon—Give it up for the guy who claps first!

Little Café Jazz 10:45 PM

A woman gets up
side aisle to leave in
midst of the Swedish jam—
tenor sax to the max, she
has this look full-up of jazz
so unlike the monk I
know the look he has
after years and years
of silent retreats
clearing his eyes
freeing his mind
to the present. Now
here's this jazz-fan
taking it all in like a
twelve-dollar glass of
Prosecco in place of you,
Jazz baby—Jasmine
jazz twins maybe
jazz jumping rope
jazz smoking dope
jazz hunched over
walker with tennis
ball feet, wheelchair
jazz and dancing in
the street, you are
dancing in your seat
as she leaves, just too
full up of festival jazz
jazz jazz jazz jazz jazz.

It Was a Cruel Summer

It was a cruel summer—
not indecisive so
much as insensitive
to our expectations.
And Jilly, though
as much a health
mentor to me
as a chiropractor
was the reason
we were all so
vigilant about
sunscreen, even
on cool cloudy days—
of which there were
way too many that August.
So to report that I was shocked
on the one hot sunny day—the day
everyone appeared wearing low cut
sleeveless sundresses, or sleeveless shirts
even at seven or eight in the evening—
to see Jilly there at the public market
covered in tattoos for Leon Russell's
concert was well, let's just say it was
a very different look—her usually
hidden heavily inked upper body.
Where's the skin safety in that?

Marianne's Consignment Shop

Marianne is like a counselor, only the
couch is her Consignment Shop counter.
I arrive with little time, tell her what it is
I can't seem to find—summer dresses with
sleeves—and she agrees that all the new
dresses are designed with younger women
in mind. I tell her that I am nervous about
next week's writing workshop, how amazing
all the teachers are. She laughs—"If you didn't
have anything to learn, we wouldn't be spending
all that money on you to go there, now, would we?"
"What?—Haha!" She slays me with the "we."
"It's so hot out," I say, as more women crowd in.
"Come on in and take your clothes off!" she laughs.
As women from the neighborhood arrive in the
old house turned second-hand shop, strangers
become sisters, soliciting and dishing advice.
Marianne, eyebrows up, wide Irish smile sighs,
"I love my job!" She says that a lot. As she gathers
and re-hangs the clothes, I wonder, does she know—
we come here for her? Her humor, kindness, care.

Marianne shares some history—"Oh, that dress just
came in today. The gal hated to give it up, but won't
wear things too many times; time to pass it on!"

I slip into the dressing room, out of the clothes I
was wearing, out of the mood I dragged in, change
my outfit, and it's great—not new, but improvised,
like jazz. I draw back the curtain for a glance in
the tall wall mirror. Marianne is out there,
like a Fairy Godmother, waving her magic wand.

Amy

This poem is not about my sister
nor is it about her upcoming birthday
It is not about the fact that I've always
envied her height. Nor is that a metaphor
for anything else I admire about her—the way
she spins her days and nights, the way she writes
so little but says so much. It is not about how she
loves her man and always has, or the way she listens
until you hear yourself when you are standing at her
kitchen's island, or sitting across from her at school,
spilling some blues only she can calm. She doesn't seek
attention, so I won't mention the way she envisions a space
in her mind long before its redesign morphs into a comfy, yet
elegant room that makes you look back when you leave it—
wondering—like you do about her—were you always there?

Mercy Me

How did we end up on that holy Vatican walkway—
on your birthday, no less—the day after mine—
mindful of the centuries gone by, the Roman
ruins, the city still partly underground, and oh my,
Michelangelo, glorious as he was—well, I wasn't sure
what it all meant to you—being brought up as a Jew.
It was never on my bucket list per se, but mercy me,
our ardent nephew, Brian, was performing
in Rome, Imola, Cento, and Salsomaggiore. Lou
and I were newly married. This was a convenient
honeymoon—to catch a once-in-a-lifetime concert
in two of the four cities. I followed all Brian's piano
rehearsals and went to high school band gigs
in Webster. We were not going to miss this.
The students were ready. The music was classical
and finely performed in gorgeous old venues with
great acoustics. The music altered time and space.
Tears stood in my eyes, during a long-standing ovation,
at the end with the Romans calling "Bravo! Bravo! Bravo!"

They clapped on and on for the Rochester Philharmonic
Youth Orchestra's regal performance. And there
was Brian, as at home on the stage as one could be.
Wanting to share the moment, I glanced around,
said to Lou "Why haven't we run into anyone we know?"
"What?" He laughed. Then honest to God—someone—
called my name, "Elaine!!"—like in the film,
The Graduate. My friend from yoga who gave me
the earrings I was wearing at that moment was there.
Now that was a Roman flourish to culminate
our spontaneous getaway to Italy.

No Faces

No faces appear in my
portrait of Montreal
taken over a three-day
vacation last Autumn.

When traveling to other cities,
I see faces of those I already know—
faces of those at home—or faces
of people I once knew, now gone.

If I see a face that reminds me of
someone—especially if it happens
twice—I imagine chances are good
that that someone is around town.

Sitting in *Cocoloco* today, facing eight
full-length windows, I see someone who
reminds me of Chuck Cuminale. "Look!" I
say to Lou as the man passes by the first four
windows. But then he disappears. He does not
pass by the next four windows. I know it cannot
be Chuck, who has passed away. Lou gently shows
me how the last four windows are really mirrors,
giving the illusion of four more windows. Unable to
speak, I think of his family: Jan, Mark, Paul, John.

On the Advice of His Doctor

On the advice of his young doctor,
to whom he complains of lower
back pain, my husband orders
online—a pregnancy pillow—
to guide him to the right and away
from sleeping at night on his belly.

The enormous, yet lightweight
package arrives, and in a few
days, my husband has learned to
sleep on his side. He's delivered
from his pain. He no longer needs
the enveloping white pillow.

His habit has changed, but
the pregnancy pillow, hangs
billowing out of an old black
ladder-back rocker in the attic—
like an unexpected guest,
come to stay for the season.

Curiously, it is this very time—
of all the times in his life
for this to happen—that
crucial information pops out of
a DNA web site—the previously
unknown identity of his mother.

Rabbit

At dawn you stare
with your side eye
facing out, not
moving across
the lawn, yet
ready to flee.

At dusk you catch
me off guard again
your stillness makes
me freeze, awaiting
movement, inevitable
change. You took Alice
to your Faerie realm
underground. She had
no appointment—or did
she? Perhaps she sent a
carrot-scented note to your
East hill side entrance hole?
You would discover this letter
later, on your time away from
the nest. You knew she was game.
She lived on the edge in a way. And
ever since Lewis reported that story,
laugh as we may, we hold our breath
when you appear, so still, just in case
you pull your pocket watch out and
find you've got pills left to share
and some Faerie realm time.

Tenth Jazz Festival/Waiting in Line

The usual greetings:
"Has it been a year already?"
"Old home week."
"See You all week!"

As we wait in line, lines we
have learned to live with at
these increasingly popular
jazz festivals, Lou sits with
the script of his first novel,
skipping ahead to the revision
of his past, changing names and towns,
changing the length of his first marriage—
I try not to read it like a memoir but it's his voice.

I'm waiting for him—not a lawyer, as in this life,
but an auditor, in the made-up book—hoping *we*
will meet in fiction as we did in real life. Why it matters
I'm not sure, but I want me, and our cat in there.
Another reader may have a different wish. Please,
make this fictional romance come true for me.

A reporter with a nice camera and manner approaches,
asks all kinds of questions: where we are from, what type
of jazz do we like, where do we park, what do we think
of the crowds, where's the best food? I get the impression
he's not one-of-us, yet, but he is very nice, and nice-looking.
I envision him, a year from now, sitting on a folding chair,
perusing the music schedule. Nearby, a contented woman
looks up from the book she is reading, my husband's novel!
They smile at each other, start comparing notes on what groups
they've heard, what to hear next, as they lose track of the time.

To the Lake

Cupping a hand over the phone,
    she'd holler to her mom,
    "Can I go to the lake?"
"You haven't done a thing
    around here today!"
 was the usual response.

Shoulders collapsed,
jaw slack, she'd yield to
whatever task would work
as tender for a free afternoon
at the lake with her friends.

Eyes rolled back, she'd moan
    into the phone, "Wait up—
I gotta do a load a laundry,"
or "Gotta wash the car—
    gimmie a half hour!"

She would slash through the
chores, as if in training, stand
rigid and tight-lipped, waiting for a nod
of release, then run, towel flying like
a flag—the mile in the sun to the shore.

Words To Go

Lori asked the hosts to pass the hat
for something she had to write after class
Eighteen writers in a room on Zoom could
certainly spare some words or phrases, even
some murdered little darlings, cut from previous
pages, edited to hell and back. Open your sack of
words you're hoarding—perhaps some triggering
places like Azerbaijan, Katmandu or Rocket Street.
Nave might keep his in a fireproof wallet; Allegra's
in a comic book vest, holding her cards to the test.
Time passes so quickly, as Terence Winch wrote
of his watch, "It ran so fast, it was always tomorrow."

Lori's friends had already left, taking the words they might
have shared back to their cars, then home, to a friend's house,
or some local bar—depending on the time zone, only to be
tossed out later by mistake, like a perfectly good dollar bill
jammed in your Levi's pocket. Take jammed! Take Levi's!
Even Monica was able to give Rachel the name "Emma"
for her newborn—a name she'd saved since age fourteen.
Now that was a gift! But you can take umbrage, voyage,
burnt umber, tossed envy, green salad, presumptuous wine.
A cocktail, "shaken, not stirred" belongs to all of us now, like
eminent domain, right? Words like A Cappella, Acapulco, razor
blade, and singed marshmallow campfire stories told again but
with a twist. See, I've got some game. Ann Patchett said that
she knew nothing about opera, terrorism, or Peru before she
wrote *Bel Canto*, but she said, "I read the New York Times." And
she has a bookstore in Nashville, where they have other newspapers,
but needed a bookstore. This needs no further explanation.

Lori, this unprecedented request of yours, well, we were touched.
You could've scanned our backpacks as we left the venue
(venue is a cool word, like genre and milieu,) but you didn't.
You asked. You asked nicely, so here you have it: free words to go.

When they test my hearing, the recorded voice offers words
for me to repeat like Sandwich, Sidewalk, Lipstick, Hopscotch.
(To that, I purposely say "Hot Doc" to amuse Mitch, my audiologist.
Two syllable hearing test words give me half a chance with the
soundproof booth, deep radio voice, space between words to pause
and think, perhaps unlike this poem, which I hand over to you now,
Lori. It's your hot potato to use or lose. Use or toss these words
on to the next lonely writer, completing their sentences
in the middle of the moonless night.

Jive Talk

Seven kids—spread out in age—
   John, Elaine, Peter, Mary,
   Bernie, Amy, Marti—
wander through open doorways:
Kitchen, Dining Room, Living Room,
   Kitchen. "Say what now?"

Someone just left the room
   as you arrived. You hear
the last two words. Or you hear
"yucky," but they said "yummy."

And so it goes; some flim flam
endless teasing first date chit chat.
We had our own Tower of Babel
   right at 44 Farrell Terrace.

"That's not what I said,"
   we still joke.
"That's *exactly* what you said,"
   the only response to that call.

Laugh-to-tears emojis replace
our carousing bodies through
door-less doorways, so long ago.
Living room, dining room, kitchen
   kitchen, kitchen, kitchen.

"I never said that."
"That's *exactly* what you said."

In Her Dream

She lies on the beach
face-up, not worried
about the sun.
It's January but
she stays active
never stops flowing—
from one project to another.

In her dream she
rolls over, falls asleep
on the beach not
worried about the sun.
She wakes up, grabs
first pen, then paper—
starts a shopping list
then a chore list,
then a list of thank
you notes to write,
calls to make tonight.

In her dream she
has fallen into a
very deep sleep
on the beach, face
to one side, her
back exposed.

In the morning,
she washes her face
opens the mirrored
medicine cabinet
catches the reflection of
her back in the wall mirror—
her sun-burned back.

His Passage

His focused breath,
        in and out
was all that held him together
as the ferry headed roughly
towards the break in his life,
        away from what
he often referred to as
        the insanity.
He was silenced by the idea
of prose flowing out of him
        like unknown prizes
        from a party piñata.

He stared out the window,
        eyes fixed on land,
the waves crashing
and breaking against
the ferryboat howled,
        "You wait."

His writer's block ended
        on Block Island,
on a sun-soaked raft
        of blessed clarity.

This poet is writing a novel.

Margot Dream

In my dream you arrive, not here
in Port Saint Lucie, nor Coconut Creek,
not Forest Hills, Gregory or Benton Street—
but back at Forty-Four Farrell Terrace, my
parents' house, our childhood home. Your
arms, outstretched offer a large metal pan of
hot meatballs. "Oh, those look heavy," I say.
"I should eat light; we're having spaghetti."
You smile, knowing they are not what they appear
to be. In a mock Italian accent, you say, "Hey, let's
eat heavy—then we can work it off." (But it sounds
like "walk it off?") Either way, you make me laugh. I invite
you and Michael, (so tall, yet sometimes invisible by your
side), to stay for dinner, knowing your dish will go so well
with Mom's special sauce. I also know they're not really
meat. I worry a little that I haven't asked Mom first.
The square walnut kitchen table seats eight at best.
Now we'll be 11, but who is missing?—and where
is Mom? Dad must be pouring wine or hanging
coats. I'm sure they'll appear soon; they love a
party! And spaghetti is everyone's favorite meal!
What happens next, in the dream, is the ultimate
tasting of the orbs you brought, which are not only
moist and warm, but light as a passing breeze
in summer. An almost translucent crispy quinoa
crust opens up to tiny white and buttery-yellow
miniature daisies, with cashmere thread-like grasses,
an other-worldly garden, sprouting and being tasted
at the same time, a mouthful of divine bounty,
never imagined or known before, yet familiar
as the kiss of one who loved you in the past.

Reorganization

I have been meaning to re-organize my
books, but how? My friend Michael files his
favorite musician's albums next to records of the
musicians he thinks they'd enjoy hanging out with.
That makes me imagine a timeless event where T.S.
Eliot meets Rumi at his *Cocktail Party*. After all,
in *Little Gidding*, Eliot meets a ghost which
is a compound of Yeats and Mallarmé. And
Rumi has written "This being human is a
guest house. Every morning, a new arrival."
Gabriel Garcia Marquez and Haruki Murikami
could discuss *Kafka on the Shore* and *Love in
the Time of Cholera*. Earnest Gaines could
share *A Lesson Before Dying* then William
Faulkner could read from, *As I Lay Dying*.
Annie Proulx might send her *Postcards*
to Carl Rogers. He had a person-centered
Way of Being. Ram Dass, upon hearing Joan
Didion's *The Year of Magical Thinking*, would
kindly explain it was all *Grist for the Mill*. Amy
Tan and Anita Diamant would have an awakening
sharing *The Hundred Secret Scents* inside The
Red Tent. Barbara Kingsolver and Michael
Talbot could dream *Animal Dreams* in *The
Holographic Universe*. Mary Oliver and
Christina Adam—would honor *Red Bird*, since
we all know, *Any Small Thing Can Save You*.

At the Strathallan

Bob grins,
ventriloquist-like,
his guitar conversing
with the band as he jokes
with the audience.
Want to sit in? he asks
the folks at the front table.

Paul Hoffman Basies the keys
as Dan Vitale bows his bass,
like a hunter, giving thanks
for a thicket of prey.
Mike Melito brushes
a breeze across
his drums—
as a river cries out
of Glasser's sax.

That'll Be the Day

Yeah, Peggy Sue—
that'll be the day—
when a guy wearing
horn-rimmed glasses,
a suit and a thin tie comes
down the line and thinks he
can be a rock star. Or maybe
he doesn't even think that at all.
Listen to me, Peggy Sue—
maybe baby, he just knows
he has a way of saying things
in a new, catchy, hand-clapping
kind of way that'll get folks up
on their feet, dancing and singing
those words of love along with him.
Maybe it's just so easy for him
somehow—like falling in love
when you're 20.   It's as if the lyrics
are just raining in his heart, every day.
What do I know. I'm just wishing
the music of a guy like that
lasts a very long time and that
his spirit does not fade away.

The Spirit

Sitting Practice

My hands have fallen apart again.
Why won't they hold together?
My bowling ball head falls towards
my chest. Hopefully no one can hear
the rattling emptiness of my groggy
breathing—as I resist the urges
to yawn, to nod, to slip to sleep.
"Wake up! Wake up!" is carved
in the block—the cracking sound
still a shock but then—all the quiet
in the room is healing to my ears,
calming my fears. I enlist my pain,
my gripes, my grief—my aging process,
at least, is clear. Yes, life is short, except
for this Teisho—which may never end.

I used to belong here—but left for some
years—returned to find myself at home—
a piece of my heart wedged deep in the wall—
the place where my focus gratefully softens.
The taiko drum's whoof resonance
still stuns, as does the rapid-fire chanting,
scents of grass mats and wafting incense.
I've missed the shared knowing and
not knowing practice between sangha
members—breathing as one, facing
Zendo walls, our own fragile walls,
letting go, coming back,
letting go, coming back,
'til time falls away.

Seventies Yoga

Today yoga teachers talk nonstop the entire class.
In the seventies, yoga teachers said little. People
thought yoga was the same as meditation,
sitting cross-legged, doing nothing.
Before there were yoga mats, we'd lay our
beach towels on sun-warmed wood floors. We'd
begin by resting in corpse pose. The teacher would
slowly coax us back up to standing, demonstrate
a pose—a pose we did last week and the week before—
with minimal guidance. We'd ease into the stretch,
releasing the day's pain for pleasure. After each pose,
we do a counter-pose. Stretching and surrendering,
dog pose/child pose, dog pose/child pose, dog/child.
Counter poses are like oyster crackers at a wine tasting.
We'd find our way, minding our breath, without
continuous instructions or complex variations.
Rest and rest from resting. Ahh, seventies yoga.
Now, in my seventies, that's the yoga I need again.
My cat Teri does Dog pose or Child Pose beneath me
when I do Dog Pose or Cat and Cow. Partner yoga!
I want a yoga teacher who is an introvert. I want
to do introvert inversions. I want to put my feet up
the wall in vipirita karani, shoulder stand for
the ill at ease—and rest quietly. I want to
return to the past to a seventies yoga class,
back before the corpse pose was scary.

Little Sentient Beings

The tiniest, most annoying insects
I've ever encountered are darting
in multiples in and around my
journal like minuscule Mexican
jumping beans on the one
nice summer night I open
the enclosed second
floor porch windows.

I plead with Lou, who knows everything, to explain why they are here.
He continues to write; I continue to ask:
Are they emerging from some decaying
pod I found on a walk and carried home
in a pocket? Or drawn to some scent?
Of what? Ink? Hand cream? A few
grains of sand still clinging to the
pile of Block Island rocks heaped in
a bowl on our writing porch desk?

They are furiously whirling around on
his work also, but he seems unperturbed,
unconcerned that they might infest our
whole house. He gets up, gestures to
me to come in from the porch.
"They will be gone tomorrow," he says.
"How do you know?!" I demand.
"I don't think their life span is very long," he says,
as he closes the door, giving them the room.

I then found compassion for their
intensity, as mine melted to sadness.

Saturday in August

The sound of a flute
floats from the park.
Nearby, two or three
lawn mowers hum and grind.
A motorcycle revs up
at an unseen traffic light.
Garage doors open along
the alley, vehicles emerge.

Zen Garden water fountain
bubbles below. Poplar
tree leaves rustle,
shimmering in the sun.

Mailbox tops snap open,
screen doors slam shut,
sisters squeal on a neighbor's
swing set. The sun silently
passes through glass panels
in a white concrete garden
bench—full of seashells—
painting white granite
stones below: yellow,
blue, green, and red.

Hoselton Toyota Waiting Room

A car dealership is a hard place to relax
It's a place of separation and worry.
As men mostly pace, women occupy
their time with reading, knitting,
or tending to their kids. The sight
of hundreds of cars in the massive lot
doesn't entice me to go for a walk.
And knowing the longer I wait,
the higher the cost might be,
keeps me on the edge of my seat.
I envision a yoga teacher in the middle
of the open space, stretching her arms up
over her head, breathing deeply, bending
forward from the waist, head hanging free.
Free loaner bikes and a bike path around
the large lot outside would be refreshing.
A Little Library would fit in here—"Bring
a Book; Leave a Book." Some grammar
school artwork would make me smile.
These car posters do not soothe me.
Oh, where is my car? My partner in
travel? There is shopping nearby—
errands stack up in my mind, but
the thing I'm without, is the thing
that I need—my car! As I wait, feet
tapping, my car is enjoying a day spa.
Finally, my name is called, my keys and
paperwork are brought to the desk—with
the ambiguous statement: *You're all set.*

Thanksgiving

"Ooh, I want to thank you for the love. Thank you for the heartaches.
Thank you for the tears I've cried. Thank you for all those lies."
 —Tony Price

I give thanks for your kindness, or cruelty.
  I give thanks for your warmth,
  or indifference. I give thanks
for what this moment must teach me.

I give thanks for early morning meditation.
I give thanks for foamy espresso coffee and scones.
I give thanks for Highland Park's amazing array of
   trees, blossoms, hills, benches, and leaves.
I give thanks for my downhill walk back home.

I give thanks for my pathologically
   happy spouse, the joy of my family,
   and cat, the warmth of our house.
I give thanks for musicians, artists,
   thinkers, and writers, who soothe
   my senses and speak to my soul.

I give thanks for children who relish life's glory.
I give thanks for the sun streaming through
   my windows this Fall morning.
I give thanks for my yoga teachers, and other
   nurturers along my life's path.
Thanks to everyone who has
ever made me laugh.

I give thanks for innumerable ways
that food can be seasoned and prepared.
I give thanks for all the recipes
my friends and family have shared.

I give thanks for those who still need me.
        Thanks to those who have let me go.
I give thanks to those who loved me and told me,
        and to those who didn't and never let me know.

I give thanks for priceless big favors
        and for everything small.
I give thanks for what I remember,
        and thanks for what I can't recall.

Scarf

He arrives,
throat aflame
wearing the scarf
his daughter made—
neither knit
nor crocheted
but woven,
on the loom
he pressed his
then-wife to give
their daughter.
She was barely
fourteen, yet
could see the warp
and woof ahead:
hollowing house
single Dad,
cold winter.

Spider

I called to Lou to come see
this big scary spider
our cat, Teri found.

(I figured he was picturing
Diane Keaton as *Annie Hall,*
when she called Alvy in the
middle of the night about
a giant spider, which was
in reality, very small.)

But Lou's eyebrows lifted
just enough to let me know
this spider really was
huge—and had to go.

In his Buddhist manner,
he cradled the fat spider
in a paper towel and gently
walked it out the front door
to set it free at the foot
of our driveway. And,
as he did so, the spider
also set something free—
her litter of tiny spiders.

What a gift from that spider
to this man who writes endlessly
about the loss of his birth mother.
This spider gave birth in his hands.

The Bikers in Montreal

I see a happiness here
I've not seen in New York
or Toronto. So many people
in the bicycle lane are smiling.
As they pass us in our cars,
(searching for a legal parking
spot), they must be joyously
reminded that they do not have
to look for a parking spot or pay
to park. They look happy, but
not in a vacation happy way. They
seem to be in their school or work
lives, but in a shared groove that
holds all the uniqueness to each
person, with their variety of ways
of dressing and somehow making
their bikes look like no one else's.
Wearing backpacks, hauling books
or groceries, even towing their kids,
these smiling moving grooving
bodies do not seem to be just
out for a ride, but they are
appreciating the ride.

Is This Time Travel Too?

The AC on the airplane is blowing
short stray hairs across my face,
triggering a memory of Dad, asking
me to pull back my hair—when I leaned
over to kiss him *goodbye* those last days
we shared. I feel bad he had to ask me
more than once. It must have been
annoying. Is this memory surfacing
here and now a form of time travel?
Was there something else?
Something beyond the surface of
that request that day back then?

The stewardess with blue eyes and
deep cheek dimples—is holding a phone
to her ear. The tone of the plane is changing.
Soon the descent will be announced, but will
take forever. She is older, maybe my age, thin
and firm. This triggers for me the one interview
I had with United Airlines—how I had to walk
back and forth, then turn around, as someone
looked me up and down. I weighed 125 pounds
at five foot seven. Not quite good enough. I'm
glad I didn't get that job, but wonder—if I had,
would I have learned to travel light and easy?
Maybe I would have been laid-off, as so many
were, and then what? Leaving my questions
up in the air, I fasten my seat belt, anxious
for a smooth landing, my life on the ground.

Trimming Privets

At the end of a long workweek,
she decided to trim the Privets
dividing two pieces of property—
hers from her neighbor's.
The more she pruned, the
more she questioned what,
exactly, they were providing
privacy for, or from? They stood
fifteen, eighteen feet tall between
a low terrace of her neighbor's yard
fronting an alley and the wall to her
own cinder block-walled garage—
private enough. She hauled out both
ladders, the long-handled tree trimmer,
a hand pruner, two rakes, leaf bags.
Every cut was a quick decision—
Don't need you! You're out! Too tall,
too intrusive, too brittle, too little, too
low-to-the-ground, too tangled in vine,
too in-my-face, too in-my-way and you
are hampering the swing of the chain
link fence gate.
Snip—
       Snip—
              Snip—
without remorse or sympathy.
This had nothing whatsoever
to do with anything else in life.

Grand

The night of the day your
conception is announced
to us, I dream—no, I *hear*
your intended gender told
to me by whomever does
the speaking in our sleep.

That voice tells me "a girl has
already started her journey,"
and unlocks a longing in me
I have not yet known.

This peanut, this peach, this
garlic bulb grows, not only in her
mother's womb, but in a space
saved in my barrenness, like
ancient Sarah—just in case,
just in case, just in case.

St. Anthony's Day

Fireworks explode—
in a clear night sky for a
new crop of kids, the way
they did when we were
there, in awe, near the
beach, not wanting
the display to end.

Quirky lake effect weather
kept us wondering all day
if the show would happen
at all. Dad hated the traffic
jams and the crowds—he stood
a head above—in so many ways.

Still, he took us down every
year at dusk, found a side street
with just enough room for his
car. We needed nothing more.

Dad seemed to savor the mandalas
of light, as they fanned and waned,
crackled and stunned. We all
dreamed in color those nights.

Desk in the Den

I have a desktop full of movie
and concert ticket stubs, art post
cards, way too many old photos,
a bowl of rocks from Block Island—
I wear the silver necklace from there
every day—a paper cutter, a Singer
sewing machine, a porcelain tray,
my spare hearing aids, two jars of
rubber cement, (one good,) a dozen
home-made birthday cards, ready to go,
my Canon Powershot camera in its case,
a yoga mat, block, and strap, some sweet
smelling sticks of incense, (gift-wrapped
by my mother, long before she died)—still
unopened, a few sketch pads—some with
Dad's cartoons, Sarah's, Eric's, Brian's, mine,
Margaret's, Lexy's—high Heveron humor, a
green painted clay frog paperclip holder, full of
straight pins fiercely facing out, a tiny red, yellow
and blue wire basket, a gift from Jaime at age 3,
a painting of four sisters from Julia, sent from
Memphis, a self-portrait of Emma from middle
school I had to have; Matt's happy big handed
snowman drawing, a 1970's Pioneer receiver,
speakers with a deep bass sound, a CD player,
JVC tape deck, mix tapes and my favorite CD's,
countless writing implements and blank journals—
all of them starving for a meaningful list poem.
But there's just no room on this old desk for that.

Kensho

A long trek to find the truth
brought me to Joe Buddha.
He could be me, an unlikely
Bodhisattva, sitting in half lotus
at the end of a lonely workday,
our eyes ahead—my checkered
past, free as the air in Kannon's
open hand as I soften—Goddess
of Mercy—finally easing up on
me—despite contemplating
those roads not taken—easing
　up on *everyone* a bit now,
　all of us getting older—
losing our former super-powers,
　like pennies falling out of a
child's torn pocket. But gaining
　the gifts of a simpler life, even
　of long silences at times,
glancing up from my book,
as you wait for a certain bird
to fly by, and just let go, easy
now, my eyelids drawing down
like a somber orange setting sun.

Trikonasana

In Trikonasana
against the wall,
I ask my inner child—
Remember going to
that doctor for posture—
exercises—was it like this?
Before I even finish thinking
the question, she reminds me
of how we went *under* anesthesia
before they took our tonsils out, and
that time we fell from the swing set, but
nothing was broken. But a week later, our
6th grade brother fell out of a tree and broke
his back. It was a stolen summer for him.   She
reminds me of the dentist who used the C *word—*
Cancer! He told us as a teen to quit smoking or else!
It was a big deal to see doctors one-on-one back then,
says my earnest inner child, my sort-of-twin, who
was *there* after all, and who enlivens each day
with her youthful energy when I welcome her
along and ask how she likes *this* moment now.
Did we ever dream of such things—a yoga
practice? Meditation? Being married?
Living in the city? How much better
it is when both of us are together.

Where Do We Go From Here?

Where do we go from here?
Clearly there has been
a glacial shift in
perspective—
ghostly faces
rise from typeset
names on the page—
or the breaking news
scrolling down my phone
for weeks and months now
leading the way to the cruel
hand of darkness. Georgia
O'Keefe's giant flowers distract
us briefly like the rising sun, like
thunderstorms and fusion jazz,
but now the sea is undeniably angry.
I can do hard things, but there are
no ropes here, no guides on the wiser
path taken by others in the past. There
is no parallel, no Google Map nor GPS to
the place we need to be. Democracy too
is slipping away like a slowly-melting
glacier: you do not see it. You do not
see anything out of the ordinary 'til
you have no other choice but to see.
Is anyone with me here? Or am I
alone on this ice hike to oblivion?

Madonna

Why are we so fearful
   of the Madonna,
   our Mother Mary,
      holding space—
Christ's own mother of
the Virgin Birth with His
   honorable father,
   Saint Joseph.

Can we not also hang our
   lariats and press passes,
   our overnight luggage—
on her outstretched arms?
She is the one who told him
"They have no more wine,"
   at the wedding feast at Cana.

Christ replied that
   his time had not yet come.
Was He truly not ready there, of all places,
and now, of all times, to turn water into wine?

His moment's hesitation is the breath we hold.
She told the servants to do as he said.
This is the son of God she is addressing,
the Lord of all, He who will be crucified
   and raised from the dead.
What was his reply to his mother?
   He did as she wished.
Imagine her warm smile.
Fear not her true-blue love.

State of Wonder

Just as I read the part about
Dr. Swenson finally appearing
out of the jungle in Ann Patchett's
book, my peripheral vision was slashed
by the sight—right outside
of my dining room window—
of a Medieval scythe being
wielded by the boy next door,
who has gone ahead and turned
into a man, over the summer.

Gabe uses the twelve-foot, curve-
bladed tool as if that was his
regular work—to hack away
at the Mulberry Bush, tall
as a Maple, whose trunk
stands firm on their side
of the fence, but whose
leafy branches block
the swath of daylight
from my sunflowers.

He leaves the fallen branches
on the ground, leaves the
shrieking gate open to our
back yard, leaves my peripheral
vision, leaves me wondering
when, exactly, he started
smiling through laborious
tasks in the heat of the day.

Double-Hung Window View

My husband's forehead is
unexpectedly reflected in
the window I am facing—
the upper frame of his
eyeglasses, his left
ear, his left arm—
This apparition
is surrounded
by snow covered
trees and rooftops
on Rockingham Street—
the blue-light icicles hang
from the front roof line of
our garage facing the alley.
In the Zen Garden below,
the Buddha is nearly
buried in snow.

A hidden sunset subtly
softens the scene—
as if my eyesight
is gradually
fading away.

Contrasts (at Lamberton Conservatory)

There are some art students here—
    adults and seniors, who take
their time sketching orchids, ferns,
    bromeliads and vines.
From this sun-soaked bench—
at a right angle to Reservoir Drive,
I face a fully bloomed red magnolia
bush growing out of soil in a pot.
Outside sits a black Civil War cannon,
aimed at South Avenue. The gushing water
fountain behind my bench muffles the sound
of passing school buses, speeding cars, and trucks.
A man, wearing an orange wool cap, propels himself
past the glass walls here with ski poles.
Next to the cannon, a multi-trunk
Maple tree hangs on to half its burnt sienna leaves.
Someone told me that Burnt Sienna and Umber
are no longer included in boxes of crayons. I
take umbrage with that! What unearthly
color has replaced them in the Crayola
army to enlist the interest of youngsters?
Soon, the doors here will be locked.
Soon, the sun will greet the horizon.
as if it was just an ordinary day.

Backyard Full

I have a backyard full of
walnuts and pine cones.
I have a backyard full
of happy squirrels. I have
a backyard full of lawn chairs
and a hammock. I have a back
yard Zen-garden with benches
and no one sitting anywhere. I
have a back yard view of a better
back yard. Nick and Nancy's
back yard gets the sun my back
yard lacks. I have a back yard full
of knowing good neighbors take care
of their sun filled garden. I have a back
yard that knows the weight of hundreds
of thousands of leaves, the price of cool
shade in summer. I have a back yard which
has a view of city lights only in Winter. I have
a back yard I keep meaning to appreciate.
My back yard boasts a water fountain.
A yellow bird bathes there each day.

Hand to Heart

You left your odd temple, the
one that met inside a church;
I left the community that was
kicked out of The Church for
following the teaching of Jesus.
Together we read aloud The Dalai
Lama's *The Art of Happiness*, a sangha
of three, two human beings, and
one cat serving as monitor, her tail
the kyosaku. Her voice breathes and
purrs its mantra, or some deep lesson
we may or may not reap before the bell
sounds. And you have found peace in
those moments that gets you through
the night and each day. You neither
resist nor brood. You allow the sitting
to wash its in breath and out breath
over your bowed head. This we
share, this practice, this space, this
quiet, this not-thinking. In the
morning you slide over to hold
me close 'til the soft chiming alarm
signals dawn. When the 2ⁿᵈ chime
sounds, you roll away, only to reach
back to take my hand in yours—
you give me the hand of Buddha
to start my precious blessed day.

Night Class

Speaking about the power of language, the teacher
suggests that even three words can change the course
of a life, such as saying "I love you." or "I am sorry."
She asks the adults in the class to come up with
other examples. One by one they respond:

"I'll call you."
"I am leaving."
"I forgive you."
"Can I come?"
"Please say yes."
"I need help."
"I need you."
"I'll be there."
"Count on me."

The teacher notices the pregnant teenager in the back
of the classroom and asks if she can think of three words.
Arlene, with one hand gently rubbing her belly, says:

"I'm keeping her."
"Her name's Vanessa."

Blues, Shoes, Unwanted News

What's That Sound?

"What is that sound?" is
a common question of mine.
"What sound?" is a common
 reply of his.
"That rattling muffle sound?"
   "Oh," he might say
"That's the refrigerator," or
"Someone is having a pool
   installed down the road."
Or "The AC just kicked on."
It boggles my mind, as the
   vibration is coming in
from another direction
to my ears, which are
working poorly at best.
Still, I ask, leaning on his fully-
 committed helpfulness,
   and over and over he
   clears things up for me.
Later, as the sun settles down,
he may ask me, "Would you
read this for me please—I
   can't quite make it out."
And so I do.
And that, my funky friends,
   is the story of a marriage
in the twilight years of life.

She Never Asked for Much

for Liz, for Lexy

She never asked for much
   but what was free—
shells from a sandy beach,
to sing a song everyone knows—

An evening walk with her man
   Elmwood to Goodman and
Clinton—to watch whatever was
showing at the Cinema Theater

To slide quietly into a pew
   in a church that felt right
in her modest clothes
favorite broken-in shoes—

A place she could volunteer
   her spare precious time
And maybe a baby, already born
   in need of a mother.

The Lounge Stage

The singer holds most of the audience
with her ample pipes, mellifluous voice,
her red strapless Christmas dress.
Yet between the stage and us,
a woman talks on and on
to the man she faces.

Even as she leans in, he
tilts back his lounge chair.
Her hands reach across
the cold square table,
his hands curl in his lap.
As if underlining each word,
her homeless fingers plead
with the air between them.
Briefly he glances her way,
then back toward the stage.

We three look away, lifting
our eyes to the shimmery
singer, her fortunate band.
"Without a doubt," my friend
says "He cheated on her."
My husband nods, "Yep,"
"it could be their last date."
I say, "It's good to be our
age." We met followimg
our life's paths. Some of
our history we share—
Some of it lies intact.

The Future Was Better

Nobody mentioned the unlikely
island of Birch trees though they
stood quietly creek-side like
unexpected tears standing
right there in your eyes
from an ancient future
we could not know—
Like when I heard myself say,
casually to a neighbor I'd only
just met: "The kids are coming
for Thanksgiving. We haven't
seen them in nearly two years!"
And there it is—like a boldface
time-lapse hypertext link, a map back
to easy street, New Year's Day, 2020, the
"kids"—Josh and Shevah leaving with Leila
and Charlie, the grand kids; we've had our hugs,
"Bye bye!" we call out "This was so much fun!"
"Yes, let's do that next time." "See you soon!" We
are booked for Leila's Bat Mitzvah, Emma & Eric's
wedding, Sarah & Joe's wedding! Three trips home—
"Bye, Bye! Bye!" we call out, waving some more
as they drive away. Who knew that, come March,
we'd all be canceling hair appointments and
house cleaners, that we'd be paying Instacart
to deliver groceries, learning about attending
events via Zoom, wearing masks or attending
doc appointments virtually. We couldn't have
imagined that thieving killer spikey virus arriving
with a swagger, only to grow roots and stay on
and on and keeping us locked down no matter
how much we begged and prayed for it to leave.

The Year That Disappeared

The year that disappeared like
hailstones, melting in Summer's
grass, has kept you close to me,
you—the one I would always choose
to spend my time with above all others—
as we, new in a community, lost the
few routines we took for granted.
We had to let slip, like torn-off
calendar pages, planned trips to
see our loved ones, and now 1,000
miles from our Zen Center at home,
we finally re-joined and committed
to daily sitting with our sangha.
Zoom was not this thing it is
now back when we took our
Buddhist wedding vows.
There would always be time for our
friends, until there was a pandemic
and everything fell apart like broken
glass, but you and I, before the sun rises,
our hands reach for each other's. And each
night, after all that has been taken, for
this, there are no words great enough.
Please accept these few words: I would
always choose to be stuck here with you.

Umbrella

Friends give me
blank journals, even
pens that light up—
to keep by my bedside.

They remind me of
the lines that drew
us together—what
we all once knew.

But that was before I was
wrestling with the wind,
clasping both fists to
my umbrella's stiff neck—
another gift she returned—
stained glass design—
holding back the lash
of a tantrum-throwing sky.

Now she walks with a walker—
in an assisted care home.
I trudge up the hill on my own.

She anxiously awaits
her earthly termination.
I offer up the terror of the storm.

Robert

Holding a candle to you my friend, burning hand
to my broken heart. And there you appear, a legend
of kindness—your minimalist smile—resigned to your
fate—just another coffee date from a million miles away.
You who took your time with every thought and uttered
sentence—you, who made sure that your dance partner
was never left wondering what's next—as you deftly led—
you with your drawl openings—looking up, rubbing
your bearded chin, you taught math to prisoners, and
helped them write poems. You wrote them letters of
farewell. The vanity license plate you scored for
your rebuilt yellow cushioned curtained
seventies van read "PEACE," and your
jaunty Rava4 read "NOT WAR."

You once taught me the Charleston as we practiced
the 4-legged moves the length of Clarissa Street, as we
left their festival. Your patience is legend. The last text
I sent you was a photo of 3 laughing skeletons sitting at a
Cantina in Florida. "This'll be us at Boulder Coffee one day,"
I wrote. "No doubt," you replied with three smiley faces—
one with stars in his eyes. You told us you would visit—
would see us "before the big holidays," you said.
How, Robert, how was I to know that would be
your last text to me before you died? Where
are you? Can you hear me in the silence?
This is so hard.
We never practiced this step.

Signs of Life

for Robert

In today's mail, Robert, from
your kind daughter—Corine
a large box arrives from a life
which used to be—the green knit
scarf you always wore—the cards
and notes we wrote while pet-sitting
each other's cats, poems I penned to
make sense of our lives or just to please.
I see you wrote one for me—but never
mailed it—who knows why—these
sweet remnants of a better time.
Your shadow led you, kept your
deep secrets, held back the ghost,
like baby tigers hidden behind a
forbidden wall. But this box recalls
our signs of life: our puns or teasing
and joking, tapes of music we loved,
fake-flirting—meeting at dance classes,
harvesting your basil plants for your first
homemade pesto, and you baking Grateful
Bread then gifting it with olive oil from the
public market, in a Guatemalan basket from
the co-op to hold more gifts, heading to many
festivals from "Lilac" in the Spring to "Clothesline"
in the Fall, and coffee dates all winter. Then, after
Lou and I moved to Florida year-round, only the
texting, until, until that window closed for good.
But now, out of the heart-fullness of your emptying
house, this undeserved gift—this box of joy returns
your duende to us for a few more precious breaths.

Healing Game

In the middle of my 48-hour
heart monitor ordeal, disbelief at
the need, we stop. "Just to get out
of the house," my husband says,
"Let's go pick-up the mail."
And there, stunningly enveloped—
the impossible embrace I need
arrives from my Dad, from DAD!
Twenty-two years in the afterlife—
as if to say, as he used to say,
"Hurts me too."

How so? You ask, as my tears
bestrew the best cards I gave him,
the only copy of a typed birthday poem
a long-forgotten scrapbook of my life's
gratitude for everything he meant to
me are here in my hands!
Reader: he saved them!

My younger big sisters took the care
and time to sort through what remained.
And like a Van Morrison song which floats
from the radio, (RADIO!) just in time to break
your shattered heart, then help you heal it, these
ancient treasures soothe my sputtering fluttering heart.

Christmas Shopping in Wonderland

It's a blizzard today, but three
doors away is a wonderland
of handmade art and crafts.
Feeling a little like Alice, I choose
a shiny brown and yellow glass
bead from an alluring assortment.
I say to Lucinda, *I know my friends by
their colors.* She laughs. I try to think
if what I just said is true. *True enough,*
I decide, happy to agree with myself.
I go on to choose purples with blues,
mauve and red with black. I find hip
and glittery gifts, even for friends
I no longer have, as I browse alone.
I avoid the table laden with cookies
and cakes, stop at the end to taste
a section of pomelo, as I cash out
and turn to leave. Richard follows
me to the door. "Did you have fun?"
he asks. I realize, just now—it's a
party as well as a sale. "Yes!" I say,
(though I don't know anyone there
except for him, and that—was long
ago.) "Aren't you staying for the music?"
"I have to get home, make dinner," I
say, as I put on my coat, hat, and boots.
"Thanks for coming over," he says.
I re-enter the blizzard, realizing
I never knew his favorite color.

September 30

for Dad

The park is shedding
its tree debris—
nuts and leaves,
twigs and seeds,
crunching under
our feet.

Sky keeps sweeping
the sun away
under its endless
tarp of gray.

But around the bend,
in a low swath
of grass, sea-lavender
crocus stand—
so sweetening
Autumn's big plans.

Nikon

I miss film.
I miss my Nikon F3.
I miss the careful capture of
the right moment, a slant of light
just before the shift in a day to the
slip of night. I miss rewinding unseen
images into a film canister, then waiting—
days and days for prints—to see how many
came out as I saw them in my mind, when I'd
pressed the shutter. I miss that deep whooshing
sound more than the heap of cash cameras cost
at the time. I miss the smile I heard in Dad's voice
when I told him I bought my first Nikon camera and
135mm lens. Oh, the portraits that lens took! Everyone
looked so great, straight-on, halting fate and time, with
their easy laughs, familiar smiles, lit from one side, so
alive! Look! See for yourself—Do you see what I mean?
Snap!

Agnes, Near the End May 2011

Four months after visiting her, for what might've been the
last time, we are honored to be able to see Aunt Agnes again.

It is Mother's Day—surely this day
she is taking some of her last
breaths, her eyes only slightly open,
as she continues to sleep the sleep
of yesterday, uninterrupted. Mary Jo
ever tenderly present, fields calls in the
hallway, prepares for the inevitable end
of this phase of both of their lives—
and for the gathering of the clan—
for the release of the breaths held-in
and welled-up tears that will surely
fall when she crosses to the other
side of that narrow hallway.
Agnes must have felt like eternity
was on *this* side the last few months—
some kind of purgatorial tarmac, or
red-tape foul-up regarding her freedom
to move on from here. Perhaps, it was the
other way around. Was she hanging back
with her dear family, not wanting to
see all their hearts so heavy at once?

In our yard, the late afternoon sun
casts a strange spotlight on the lone
Bleeding Hearts standing tall amongst
the gang of shaded Pachysandra,
lying low, in their usual places.

Hospice Care—January 3, 2015

I sketch my mother lying in bed here,
her mouth open, head facing left,
her throttling throat's congestion
sputtering sound, then stopping,
quiet, silent 'til the rumbling rises
again. The sketch is hard for me
even as I feel her peacefulness. I
need a last look at her; it's just Lou
and me here now. I can't very well
pull out my phone camera as she
slips away from us. Marti gave
me pad and colored pencils. I
never bought any for me before—
always preferring bright
bold markers, but how
perfect they are for today—
Mom is done saying things like
"How do I look—Is this scarf okay?"
She always looks perfect, even now.
On and on she sleeps the grateful sleep
of one whose unbearable pain has finally
been expelled. Was that Christmas day
photo the last one then? Again, I pull out
my sketch pad and keep drawing, for Marti
for all my siblings, for when the rumbling
breath finally lets go, moments from now.

Attic Full

I have an attic full
of a space trying
not to be an attic. I
I have an attic full
of hot air in summer,
cold air in autumn.
I have an attic full of
angles. I have an attic
full of the silence that
only the third floor knows.
I have an attic full of photo
albums I no longer open. I
have an attic full of clothes from
whatever season is not now. I have
an attic full of old dolls our grand-
daughter, Leila lays down on the
thick green carpet. She covers
the dolls with terrycloth squares,
saying good night to each one.
Then, squealing with laughter,
she tosses the washcloths
over the short attic wall,
down the staircase to us.
I have an attic full of echoes
of Leila's fleeting childhood.
None of us knows this day her
"only child" status is about to
change. Her brother Charlie
is on his merry way to us all.

Six Doors From Oncology

Our street dead-ends to the Oncology
Department at Highland Hospital.
This morning you stood outside the side door entrance,
to Oncology, smoking cigarettes in your scrubs!
What would make you see the irony here?
How do you get to have a job there?
If I had a Polaroid camera, I'd take your picture
smoking in front of that Oncology sign, and hand it to you.
Would you cough out a *Thank you* or toss
the photo on the butt-littered sidewalk?
Would you say, *Mind your own business*, in your gravelly
voice as you waved the smoke away from your face?
Or would you ask me if I ever smoked?
I would say "Yes. Two packs of Kools a day for 15 years."
How did you quit?
"I just quit."
Was it hard?
"Well, I lost my job and my marriage ended around then."
Then what?
I found another job and moved on."
Do you ever miss smoking?
"No."
Do you wish you had never smoked?
"Yes."
Why do you care about me—a stranger?
"Because we're all part of a whole; we're all one.
And you're killing yourself."

Osama Bin Mouse?

As I listen to the news of the capture
and death of Osama Bin Laden, our cat
Mystie races into the kitchen, loudly
announcing some big deal of her own—
then drops on my Pakistani rug, a black
furry pink-eared mouse, belly-up, its
little white sales tag intact, its
red felt eyes wide open. I pause from
breakfast to acknowledge this—
"Good job, Mystie!" She stalks out
of the kitchen. I try to recall this new
looking three-color mouse. I wonder,
if we gave it to her for Christmas,
where has it been all these months?
Was it hidden in the unused fireplace?
I wonder why she chooses, on *this* day,
to drag him out of hiding and what,
if any, repercussions there may be.
I dip the nose of mouse into some catnip,
lay it on the living room floor, near Mystie.
To my amazement, she does not move. She
glares at me.   This is not a toy; this is not
a game. I'm not sure what to do. Two hours
pass as she lies still, her back to the mouse.
Finally, I cover mouse with a cloth. Mystie
cries out three times. She remains on
the floor, with her back to the mouse.

The Darkness of Night

Like a mission of mercy,
   relief and hope arrive
as the sun sets. Darkness
brings truth and forgiveness.

A blackening sky allays our fears
for a few blessed hours each night,
as we each ease out of our armor
into loosely fitting night clothes.

All of us: grownups, babies, teens,
nuns, murderers, thieves in their
prisons, elderly folks—perhaps
for the last time—slip under our
   own healing carpet of stars,
leaving the racetrack of day,
plundering business, dirty
jobs, staggering streets—
to clear out, to cool off,
to breathe, skin to sheets,
eyelids shut, allowing our
unconscious to conduct an
unwritten symphony of night.

Walking in Montreal

I get caught up in the idea
of capturing Montreal through
the shoes people wear in the street,
in Park du la Fontaine, in Mt. Royal
Park, as well. I try to make it a critical
parameter to photograph peoples'
shoes without them knowing
I am doing so—quickly, as I
walk by, as they walk by, or
as I pretend to be shooting
something else. Only twice
do I ask permission—of the
mothers of two toddlers.
Both times, I am surprised
at how long after the photo is
taken, those children continued
to stare me in the eyes, as if to say,
"who are you?" I bow to them,
and say, "Merci beaucoup," which
makes them laugh. Even children
recognize a poor accent. Every
single person in Montreal seems
to be wearing a different pair
of shoes, as surely as each
person has a different face.
In my photos, of this trip,
no faces are shown. In my
memory, two toddlers
stare back at me, then laugh.

Twelve Below Zero

The last Christmas card of the year arrives,
hand-made, a panoramic Winter-scene
photo, Lake Placid, aptly named it seems,
a few mountains, blue sky, some
hazy sun, snow-dusted evergreens.
"12 below zero," you noted on the back.
"Don't you miss winter?" the quietest
friend I have wrote inside, above
the cheery red Christmas wishes.
"Well, yeah," I want to say, "The winter
you love," as I recall a rented skating rink
one birthday, you gracefully skating
with ease, pleasing your many guests.
I was honored you intrepid hikers kept
including me in invites for all day
snowshoeing or kayaking, followed by
pot-luck dinners, (although I mostly
came for the potlucks and company.)
You brought home-made dips and
warm made-from-scratch crackers.
You saved your sad news for the back
of the card, ". . . We're getting
a divorce, she says that . . ."
God, it felt like the last straw in a year
of continual losses—shared in
longhand—carrying the sadness of
every town it passed along the way.
Yet your reaching out lifted me up.
We carry one another in our hearts.

My Memory is 99% Full

My phone's memory
holds over 1,000 videos
now, even with the eight
out of ten I delete each day.
Snapshots are easier, like the one
I sent to my sisters and brothers
last night—December full moon
back lighting clouds in a royal sky—
a goodnight kiss from the southernmost
state. Their response is all I ever need.

Dad bought me my first camera—a Brownie,
when I was nine. He was 38 and more handsome
than Paul Newman or George Clooney—and he
walked me around the neighborhood, helping me
find the first photo to take on the roll and to not
waste film. A landscape shot—Mt. Airy—from Saint
Paul Boulevard—in black and white. It was nice!
But I missed the perfect shot, as I so often do—
he was standing right there by my side.

February: Mary Jean's Month

I do not long for the shortest month to end.
My best friend was ushered into this world
in February—the month of Valentines—her
red hair—some kind of party flag, those
flashing green eyes—like Brenda Starr.
Until I was seven, I was encircled by my
brothers, older, younger, John, Pete,
and 5 more neighborhood boys.
The day Mary Jean and I met, my father
took a snapshot of us—we were already
laughing; she had a fun-factor perspective.
I trusted her completely and immediately.
We were our mother's helpers as we
became big sisters to new siblings, five
times for me, eight for her. Meanwhile, we
found time for badminton, ping-pong, cheer leading,
swimming, cartooning fashion, baking, writing. We
walked and biked all over town, learned to dance,
learned to date, learned to drive. She starred in both
our high school musicals. We all swooned. After
graduation, we both moved away but stayed in touch.
As a nurse, she made everyone feel better with her
her gorgeous confidence, her mile-wide smile, her wit.
She was born in this month of snowstorms, cold wind
and long nights. One day before her 47th birthday,
she passed away breaking all our Valentine's hearts.
Today the temperature rises just enough
that defrosting ice streams tears
down the folds of cold lawn
furniture covers. I wait for a sign—
a cardinal, a red berry—anything.
I know she's around somewhere.

Dad's Letters

Yesterday I finally read my father's letters from the 1970's I've been saving in a bottom dresser drawer all these years. It was the 22nd anniversary of the day he died. My first impulse was to scan them to send to all my siblings. But then I realized I could not. Not yet and maybe never. They are so deep in my heart right now. His love was unconditional, and his compassion was so great. Every day without him is full of emptiness and yet full of his ever-burning light, his care and kindness, his humor and joy. Many a time he has rescued me from sadness or hopelessness from his side of the thin veil between worlds. He has flown me far above this precious earth to remind me of its beauty. He knows I know it will end one day. I told him once that when he went it would be unbearable. Without pause, he replied, *"You too, kid."* And that from a man who avoided the subject. He would say he'd learned something from experience and then, smiling, point out that he had not used the word *"age."* How did I ever move to Florida for ten years when I could have kept seeing him more often? He once said that, although he got that it was cold in Rochester and Florida was a draw for me, when the war was over for him and his peers, *"We just wanted to go home."* And I get that, maybe now more than ever, away from my family, my third move to Florida.

Cutting

I am trying
to root
the Vinca
trimmed from
my father's
grave.

I am trying
to keep
it alive,
but it seems
to have
other
plans.

Car Karma

In her youthful drives
she takes chances, taps
a Kool cigarette out of its
hard pack, yanks and strikes
a match, lights it, forgetting
the road, as a burning ash
drops to her lap, or a spark
flies up.   She steers the car with
her thumb and two fingers—as
the driver ahead suddenly comes
to a stop. A pedestrian appears,
like a character who was not in
the story, but now is the lead guy.

Even now, decades later, her heart
pounds, when she awakes, startled,
from a smoking-and-driving dream—
the car ahead stopping, the match,
the ash, the pedestrian, the brakes.

She doesn't smoke anymore.
But who does? Hardly anyone.
Now, everyone is on their phone.
But she cautiously minds the road,
both hands on the wheel, a bit
concerned about her karmic deal.
Are the hands of fate locked? Are
there more startling stops ahead?

Before and After; Last and First

In the first three months of Mom's life,
Women did not have the right to vote.

After Mom's last breath
A trailing past began:
Last phone call from Mom,
Last cards we sent her, still tucked
   in their slit-open envelopes,
Last Christmas with Mom,
Last Party at The Landing,
   all of us dancing—
Last photos with Mom—
Last tender thank you notes she wrote—
   still on the round wood table.
Then the reverse:
First return home from a trip—
   without a phone call to Mom—
First photos I can't pull from my purse to peruse
   while we wait for her doctor or nurse,
First concert I cannot describe for her—
First film I can't entertain her with—
First news article she'd already have read
   when I called to get her perspective.

First election, always so close
   to her birthday—
Are you watching, Mom?
Will we have a woman president?

Across a Downtown Street

She wears a brown sheer glittery
blouse, a batik skirt with uneven
hem, a worn-out pink fleece
hoodie—nothing makes any
sense to my eyes. Nearby, a
boy bounces up and down,
chattering nonsense. She shrugs,
nods, now and then, says nothing.
You want to give her something,
but what? A compliment?
No. You do not exist.

You could stare at her
all day and she'd never notice—
never look over. Eventually
a bus swallows her whole.

Later, in your dream, she
walks three blocks home from
a bus stop, unlocks a solid wood
door, steps out of her shoes, peers
into a near-empty refrigerator, nods
slightly, as if in agreement, then climbs
into bed without removing her makeup
or clothes. She does not turn off the light,
but the room goes dark as she falls off to sleep.

For Kelly

It was Mother's Day—
Your mom, my brother and you
were enjoying a beautiful drive.
Patti was noticing the details
along the way in Chesapeake Bay,
but that day the thoughts she tried
to share tumbled down the stairs
between her brain and her mouth.
She tried to say that her words were
jumbled, but like fingers pressing
the wrong keys, she stumbled.
But you, my hero, you made a
"you turn"—You drove to a
Firehouse. Paramedics took over
for the angels who got you there—
(their wings hiding the pearly gates.)
They pointed, like Scarecrow, to the
right hospital—the Good Witch place.
Somewhere between OZ, home, and
a very big storm, neither a dream
nor a nightmare—you—Kelly,
saved your mom's life—
on Mother's Day—not with
a champagne brunch, not with
flowers or a new blue scarf,
but with your brain, my dear—
your brain, and your precious heart.

Storm Forecast

We're finally going to *get ours.*
The foot or more of snow
forecasters predict for
Rochester looms over us
like the imagined fist
of a schoolyard bully.
We have been lucky
so far this winter, some
would say. While other
cities got clobbered by
Mother Nature, we've
been tiptoeing around,
hoping she wouldn't notice
our only average snowfall,
our only average cold, the
nice thin ice. From where
I sit inside, it is unusually
quiet. I can see a couple of
cars crawl down Rockingham
Street, but I cannot hear a thing.
A dozen or more sparrows hop about
inside a thorny metropolis of a Barberry
bush. The bamboo-covered chain-link
gate to our garden is already ajar from
a heap of last week's snow—piled up
against it. It is now late in the day.
The expected *Storm* arrives tonight.

Hermit Crab

Liz's uterus, stretched to
the size of a football, holds
a strange mass. Her doctor, still
in scrubs and surgeon's cap, spills
her fear: concern that this tumor
is a rare, aggressive cancer, may
already have spread to a lung.
One or two sentences—half a
minute; a world no longer the
same as it was. We blink back
tears, glance at one another
helplessly, blurt out our few
questions as they bubble up.

Two weeks later, at the pet store
Liz says to the clerk, "We're not
having very good luck with our
hermit crab. Should we change
the water more often than once a
week? Every three days? They like
humidity, right? I keep the top propped
open a little. Should I let him out of the
cage more often? He seems to really like
that. They are social, right? Maybe having
another one will help? Some people say
they live for years, but ours seem to only
last a few months. What should we do?
What should we do differently now?

I Choose a Jester

At the Memorial Art Gallery
I walk across the front of the grand
old building, past the metal penguins,
the shiny silver cubes, the abstract dancers,
through the tall glass doors, past the indoor
sunken sculpture garden, then up the stairs
to a third-floor office. I stand amidst a small
collection of prints, available only to patrons,
in return for our past support. From the
vast array of artists, whose various styles hint
at the gallery's collection, I get to take home
one free print. I look, browse and peruse,
then choose this odd jester or clown.
He is depicted neither happy
nor sad—but strikingly neutral,
open and calm. The clerk packs
my print in a cardboard sleeve
and nods me a kind dismissal.
One second out the door, I pass
in the hall an uncanny female version
of the joker in my print. She, in her
puffed polka dot outfit, looks me straight
in the eyes, pauses, as if to ask, *why him?*
She then disappears to my right.

Love Poems, Used

Who parted with that little book—
Who left such a thing at Barnes
& Noble's Second-hand Section
for someone like me to find?

It's so slim and square
a book—still with the dust
jacket on—protecting its
armored red cover.

For three winters it has
laid on my nightstand
awaiting my interest.
I couldn't get past the cover—
Love Poems, Used $5.00

Today, only because it's
Valentine's Day, and I
have nothing else to give,
I crack the book to find
this inscription inside:

"Big Kiss, Baby—Happy
    Valentine's Day!"
with a perfect lipstick
kiss impression beside it.

My Feet, My Love

In real life my feet ache
and love is perfectly sane.
In my dreams, my feet are
pain-free, but love is strange.
Sometimes my feet run
ahead of me down the street
in the last dream of the night.
I try to lasso them back, my
thoughts unleashed to the
gulf between night and day,
like a popped-open dream
suitcase, strewing everything.
As I lie embraced, my back to his
chest, I tell my dreams to my love,
who stars in them as an odd blend
of himself and other men I've known.
Bemused, he tells me *his* dreams
are routine, like filing paperwork,
or that he has not dreamed at all.
I envy his *off switch*—he can shift
straight to sleep, despite what the day
gave to him, or what it took away.
Awakening, I watch my legs merge with
my aching feet, as they slide into slippers.
They want to stay there, so I offer as
bribes: ice, Arnica lotion, thick socks,
soft shoes, promises of massage,
and love that is sane in the day.

Shopping for Two

There is only one woman ahead of me
in line at Tops grocery store, but there
are two piles of groceries, divided
alongside her. I reach for a
separator as I load mine
onto the conveyor belt.
She smiles apologetically,
"I'm shopping for two."
I notice a similarity to
the items my mother used
to ask me to pick up for her:
a few slices of roasted turkey
from the deli, two bananas, a
Tropicana orange juice, some bread—
"Shopping for your mom?" I ask.
"My Dad," she says, making a face—
"Half of this will go to waste," she says,
shaking her head, as her overloaded
keychain drops to the floor. I dive
down, pick it up, hand it back to her.
I don't ask her father's age, or if he
lives nearby at The Meadows, as Mom
did for so many years. I don't ask if he
keeps up on the news, uses a walker,
or if he still remembers her name. I can't
seem to speak. But, as she leaves, I hold
my hand up to my heart, my key ring, with
only two keys now, hangs from my finger.

Your Call

Your call is very
important to me.
Press ONE if you love me
Press TWO if you have a
  question about love
Please remain on HOLD
  (forever) if you intend
  to break my heart.
If you can't recall the
  options, press THREE
and go back to the start.

You Left

You left my heart homeless.
How dare you leave me here—
alone to row the waters we
once so sweetly shared?

Oh, that's right—
You can't say *love*
or *heart* in a
poem today.
You have
to show,
not tell,
not say.

Funeral Escape

Under a flock of giant
  black umbrellas,
cigarette smoke wafts,
  while grown siblings,
no longer in the habit of
hanging together fidget,
  stare at the sidewalk.
Anger pokes at the overcast
sorrow, the shared grieving
outside the funeral parlor.
They almost didn't notify him
when their mother passed.

Someone, an outsider,
offers glasses of water,
offers to make reservations
for dinner. "How many
want to go? Who wants
to get away from this?"
Softly someone asks:
"Can we?"

The Food and Other Pleasures

Cheesy Eddie's

It's still mid-October, but temps
are already down in the thirties;
a needle piercing rain rushes us as
we walk around the neighborhood.

We head down Averill Avenue from South.
Cheesy Eddie's back door is wide open,
a screen door flapping like it's Summer.
Inside, a woman wearing a sleeveless white
t-shirt under her chef's apron stands facing
three giant blocks of cheese—the size
of cases of wine—waiting like marble
for Michelangelo's hands to begin.

Cheesy Eddie's has been around
since the seventies so I know I can
buy a slice anytime, but I never do.
I don't know why but those deep
creamy top-toasted pie/cakes
are over the line for me. One
has to say no to something.

In New York City once, my mother
got the recipe for Lindy's Famous
Cheesecake. She simply asked, and
someone wrote it out for her in
longhand like she was family. So
rich! Twenty-three eggs! Cream!

But that gal on this freezing
morning with her bare arms—
facing the long day ahead
stays in my mind like the
photo I wish I had taken.

What I Remember

Every year the mammogram pre-exam
paperwork lists the same questions—
Have you ever had this or that? Have
your mother or sisters had breast cancer?
Every year I call my mother to ask how
old she was when she had her mastectomy.
Each year "seventy," sounds younger to me.

I do not remember which breast of mine
a doctor cut open to remove a benign cyst.
I *do* remember the sandwich my mother brought
me from Oscars Deli when she picked me up from
the hospital: sliced tomatoes and avocados, sunflower
sprouts, Provolone cheese, and mustard on sourdough bread.
I do not remember the level of pain or the number of stitches.
but I can still see the party toothpicks holding the sumptuous
sandwich fillings together. I can still taste the salty, thick, crisp
potato chips, and the first quenching sip of effervescent ginger ale.

I remember the tone of my boyfriend's voice, who found the
pea-sized lump when he asked, "What's this bunny-girl?"
After surgery, he did not bring me flowers, but I laughed
aloud when he handed me a tiny purple silicone Popsicle. He
also brought three coffee-table sized art anthologies. We sat
in glider chairs on the porch of Benton Street as he turned the
pages of those books until I was tired enough to
sleep and dream in modern art scenes.

They do not ask for these details on the form.

Isn't It Rich

for Bernie

Thanks for the hummus, Bernie. Unlike the creamy grocery
store kind, you could tell it came from chick peas. The story of
loaves and fishes kept coming to mind, as my add-ins kept
your bowl of hummus almost always half-full. I added some
olive oil the first day, as you suggested, good idea. The next
day, some lemon juice, a little tahini, pepper and cumin—
even thought it was perfect, exactly as you made it.
(I've ruined a few dishes by adding too much. But your
hummus was un-ruin-able.) I spread the hummus on a
whole grain bagel one day, added mild banana peppers
on top of that, like we used to do on Fridays in the coffee
room at Xerox. Another day, I added basil pesto on top
of the hummus on a thin whole wheat bun—my favorite
sandwich to-go. I diced a sweet red pepper and added
that. I chopped a bunch of cilantro in the food processor
and mixed that into the hummus. So healthy and good.
I spread your gift of hummus on rice crackers and on
toasted pita bread. It nicely filled up scoop-style corn
tortilla chips too.

Tired after a whole morning of being on my feet, I ate
the last of it today—the eighth lunch from your home-
made hummus. I ate it with Sarah Vaughan singing
"Send in The Clowns" on the stereo in the great room.
I was reading Leonard Cohen's poetry book,
Stranger Music, all the while appreciating you.

I Never Said That

I never said that!
That's exactly what you said!
Did Mom and Dad know?
It was Saturday night; they were out.
They *never* went out.
They *always* went out.
Where was I?
You weren't born yet.
We always made fudge
when they went out.
And they figured it out?
Yes! But how? We washed
the pans and dishes!
They probably smelled it!
Oh, I never thought of that.
Maybe they didn't care.
They cared when John and I
both stayed out past midnight.
At 3:00 AM; every light in the
house was on. So Grounded!
Mom used to say, "We can't sleep
'til we know you're all safely home."
Dad would say, "And then you wake us up."
Remember the giant mud turtle?
Was that when Dad jumped in the pond?
No, he went in after Pete when
the ice broke in the woods.
Where was I?
How old were we then?
I don't remember.
We were kids.

Warm Nights (9 Imaginary Future Post Cards)

Friday, August 24
Back in the Grove—*Happy Note*—
Our former store—going out of
business—all LP's $3.92, our old
price stickers! *Misty.*

Saturday, August 25
Remember hanging at Bayfront Park
shelter? Ganja galore—free live music
That infrared purple tree photo I took
there? They charge admission now!
Rainy, Off and On.

Sunday, August 26
Coral Gables Miracle Mile w/all the
shi-shi shops out of $ range. Skyscrapers
now—banks, brokers. No soul.
Slightly Chilly.

Monday, August 27
Hey—Le Jardin Bistro—still here!
All our birthday dinners with those
glass coffee cups! (My Milt & your
Steven now gone.) *Unbearably Humid.*

Tuesday, August 28
Always loved driving thru royal
palms to Key Biscayne beach.
Sign says "*Mosquitos are bad.*"
Duh!! Never had patience 2 lie
in sun. Even now. Remember
that lifeguard though? *Hot.*

Wednesday, August 29
Remember people used to
call Miami a "cultural wasteland."
Opposite now, insane. Slick.$$$
No funk. *Stifling.*

Thursday, August 30
Cheers from "Last Carrot"—still
w/the carob rice cakes, sunflower
butter. Remember how they
always put purple cabbage in
the pitas, even when we asked
them not to? Same employees!
Still cheerful. *Perfect Temp 2day.*

Friday, August 31
Guess where we are! Stubs
on the floor—Yes! Jai Alai! The
fastest sport! Cubans still yell at
all their favorite players. Oddly
exciting. Window bet takers
give slow change from a $20.
Holding my purse in death grip.
Warm Night; Full Moon.

Saturday, September 1
Ah—La Cinema d'Arte—still here,
but cut into three parts: one foreign,
two indie screens. Everyone stays
through credits. I never get over leaving
freezing AC at 10 PM to 73 degrees
outside. *That* is what I loved about
Miami. *Breezy.* See you soon. xox, e

Flowers to a Party

The thing about bringing a vase
of fresh-cut flowers to a party
   is that they get to stay—
unlike a tray of olives or cheese,
which leaves at the end, half-spent.

A flower-filled vase arrives
unexpected—a bright and
special guest of a guest,
   she herself beaming
her huge half-moon smile.

After the party, the flowers witness
the hosts congratulate each other with
kisses, as they dance in the kitchen
while doing the dishes, warmed
by new neighbors, old friends.

Days later, still-fragrant orange tea roses
and bobbing white daisies are cut back,
moved to an Ikebana vase with fresh
water—as if to finally sit down and say,
"Hey—what a great time we had, huh?"

October Walk

All day I could stare
at this giant tree I pass—
folding left in the breeze,
its dozens of shades
of green spellbinding
as a crackling fire.
Blue jay twitters by
at eye level—showing
off? Seeking edible
berries or seeds?
A huge black beetle
crosses the asphalt like
a sniffing bloodhound.
I squeeze my long-
handled tongs,
continue my task
of removing debris
from the path, curious
about the half dozen eggs,
the pink cotton bra, a nearly-
empty bottle of beer, crushed
pack of Newport cigarettes. I
try not to envision everyone else
who shares my so-called secret path.
There are other deer in the forest, Bambi.

Pelican Pair

As if to help us settle in
to our Coconut Creek home,
a pair of pelicans appear at the pond—
the little lake we view from our patio,
the lagoon with its glittering fountain,
lit up after dark from under the water.

Lou names one of them "Scott Pelly-can,"
after the newsman we watch at night,
and the other one, "Nancy," the field
reporter for whom he seems to light up.

It is Daylight Saving Time now, so
sunsets follow the news as amateur
fishermen stand at the water's
edge with their poles and pray.

By turn, the pelicans lift into the air,
their six-foot wingspan stunning—
soar around the arc of the pond, once,
twice, briefly sweeping out of sight,
then return to dive like bowling balls
bombed from clouds—breaking the water's
sleek surface, submerged, then jauntily jerking
the short jaw of their deep beaks. They spew
out excess water, swallow the menhaden.

Outshone by the pelicans' magnificent
display, the humbled fishermen
pack up their gear and bait,
head out and call it a day.

Taos, Sunday July 14th

Bowl of whole walnuts,
uncracked, half glass of
water, sits on the table.
Suzie naps as Pete plays
piano. Lou stares at the
computer screen, reading,
deleting our junk-mail.
Beyond Taos mountain,
the wide-open sky darkens.
Wind, all hepped-up over
a looming rainstorm,
whines like an Oxo tea
kettle, through a window
barely ajar. All three dogs
and both cats doze in their places
One hummingbird, having fought
the others off, flits like a sommelier,
from one plastic feeder to another,
rating the sugar water. We've taken
our sunrise walk, gone to church,
met the pastor, had our New Mexican
lunch at "Orlandos," heard the poets,
singers, and renowned artists.
We have bought our Taos
gifts and tees. And now—
must we leave?

Retirement Projects

Large sketch pad in hand, I stand,
in the classroom, lightly marking
the paper with my graphite pencil. I do
not glance at the other students' work—
to check how much more advanced they
must be than me, as this is only my first
live figure-drawing class, and I can't be
comparing. I'm anticipating my return
to the sewing project which scarfed-up
my entire weekend, including all chores.

In this drawing class, there are three or four
plates of home-made cookies, chips, scones
and pink lemonade laid out directly below
a sign that reads, *Absolutely No Food
in the Painting Room*. The words on
the sign are framed with tiny sketches
of ants and Palmetto bugs. Two hours
later, after leaving for the day, (and, as it
happens, the year), I regret not having taken
a snapshot of that sign behind the snacks.

Back at the condo, I adjust the Singer sewing
machine's light, re-fill a bobbin, but see now
that I'm distracted by the thought of a poem
I want to write about sewing—how it seems
that some fabrics sail through the machine like
grateful last-minute dinner guests—yet other
fabrics are testy or wiggly, as if not sure that
they agree to the weight of the thread, the length
of the stitch, or the idea of being here at all.
Did they think the remnant pile was forever?

Return to Boulder Coffee

Here's what you don't realize
you miss until you return:
sunlight and huge sky—
to the North, to The East,
even to the West. Polished
round knotty-pine tables,
shiny and clean, with room to
spread out the whole newspaper.

You can see Xerox, Bausch & Lomb
and Lincoln Tower in the distance.
Four red maple trees patrol the
corner of Alexander Street and
Clinton Avenue. Orange construction
cones and barrels do not seem to
slow traffic, nor hamper the flow
of pedestrians or bikers. A cartoony
painting of Uma Thurman hangs by
the patrons absorbed in a wild variety
of music. Oh, but the thing you came in
for: the richest roasted coffee in town.

She Lived in Two Houses

She lived behind me in
two houses on Beaufort
Street. She went to sleep
and woke up in one, then in
the morning she crossed the
lawn, unlocked the door to her
second house, struck a match,
placed a tea kettle on the gas stove,
poured milk and cereal into a bowl.
In the Summer she worked in her yards.
We talked about pruning roses, the cost
of groceries and heat, neighborhood gossip.
Standing on opposite sides of the pine back fence,
we ate our sandwiches together sometimes.
I was thirty-five and she was seventy-eight
years old the day she told me all nine of
her siblings had passed—her brother,
who owned the breakfast house—was
the last to go. I noticed the safety pins
holding her housedress together and
asked her a personal question—"Why
not sell one of the houses—wouldn't
it help, you know, with the bills?"
She shook her head, "You don't
understand sentimentality, dear—
when everyone is gone, you hold
on to the things that held them."

Is This Better?

How did you first react
to computer jargon—
terse Morse code, data
flashing without a sub-
text to read. How easily
did you tune in to the new
wavelength—original words
now blip-talk and code rap.
"Is this better?" I often wonder
about technological advancement.
Take, for example, the many minutes
it seems to take a waiter to punch all
the keys required to order a sandwich,
the ensuing useless foot long receipt they
hand you, versus the 10 seconds it takes
to jot down 3 or 4 words, with a pencil,
on a handy 3" x 4" pad, then call out to
the cook, "Egg salad, hold the fries."
This is my internal quibbling brain—
which is better I ask you, in the
case of lunch. I know. I know.
We wouldn't even be here in
the writing group right now,
various time zones, full color
and sound, to share this hour
if it weren't for the evolution of
data processing, but not every
single thing must go this route—
please, at least, not the sandwich.

Avoid Dance

I sew to avoid writing.
I meditate to avoid thinking.
I do laundry to avoid cleaning.
I read to avoid ironing clothes.
I play music to avoid going out.
I make popcorn to avoid cooking.
I shop online to avoid paying bills.
I rake the leaves to avoid walking.
I prune plants to avoid socializing.
I watch TV to avoid returning calls.
I make lists to feel organized.
I list only what I accomplish.
Today I completed a list poem.

Poetry Is Not

Poetry is not memoir.
Poetry is not a homily.
Poetry is not a warning
nor admonition.
It is not a lecture,
nor should it be.
(Heh, heh.)
Poetry is not a resume
nor recommendation letter.
Poetry is not an invoice,
but might be a statement.
Poetry is not discriminating;
it is wheelchair accessible.
Poetry is not authoritative,
though it should ring true.
Poetry is not a tow-away zone
thought it may be in *some* zone
to which you've been transported.
Poetry is environmentally friendly—
if not disposable—at least recyclable.
Poetry is not one size fits all—but
you are welcome to try it on. Feel
free to say you heard it from me,
Here's a copy of my poetic license.

Sweet Dreams

I knew you once.
Still think of you.
That time we spent
More face to face.

It is quite late—
Not much to say.
No clever words.
No plea, no case.

I knew you once.
Still think of you.
That's all I'll say—
Yeah, you!

Acknowledgments

Thank you to Stuart Glazer, retired Florida Atlantic University Chair of Music Department, composer, painter, and friend, for the cover artwork, *Girls Night Out*.

Thank you to Allegra Huston and James Nave, authors of *Write What You Don't Know*, for their original Imaginative Storm method of writing: https://imaginativestorm.com. Many a Saturday, Lou and I join their Taos-based group via Zoom, along with writers from around the U.S and beyond. Using their wildly unique visual prompts, we quickly jot down words that come to mind, creating a shared list. Then, like speed-chess players we write for just ten minutes. What comes out of these sessions are jaw-droppers and revelations. Thanks to what I gleaned from them, I've refreshed the way I think, write, and rewrite. Editing this collection was a joyful blast.

Thanks to my sublime six siblings, extended family and dear friends who kindly read my early drafts when I can't wait to share them.

Thank you to Sheila for introducing me to Lou, and for always being there for us no matter where we all are.

Thanks to the Rochester Zen Center, especially for keeping morning zazen going, during and since Covid via Zoom. Thank you for Buddha, Dharma and Sangha.

To the grieving families of our recently lost dear friends, Jacqueline Lindauer, Robert Nenno, and Tim Sullivan, I give you my heart.

About the Author

    Elaine Heveron grew up in Rochester, NY, graduated with the pioneer class of Bishop Kearney High School and graduated from Villa Maria College in Beffalo. She has two previous collections of poetry, *Email to Cleveland* (2007) and *Not Every Woman Swooned* (2009,) both published by Plain View Press, and a chapbook, *Standing Room Only in My Heart*, published in conjunction with Goose River Press. She and her husband, Louis Faber now reside in Port Saint Lucie, Florida with their amusing, smart, energetic, and joyous cat, Teri.

Printed in the USA
CPSIA information can be obtained
at www.ICGtesting.com
LVHW050820170923
758370LV00003B/4